My eXtra Special Brother

Stephanie ♡

eXtra love
Carey
Scott
☺

My eXtra Special Brother

How To Love, Understand, And Celebrate Your Sibling With Special Needs

Written by
Carly Heyman

Illustrated by
Stephanie Conley

My eXtra Special Brother
Written by Carly Heyman
Text © 2003 Carly Heyman
Illustrations © 2003 Stephanie Conley

First Printing
January 2003

Library of Congress Control Number: 2003101010

Trade Paper Edition ISBN 0-9727865-0-3
Hard Cover ISBN 0-9727865-1-1

Cover photography and photograph on page 92 by
Warren Bond Photography

Book and cover design by Martha Nichols of aMuse Productions

Printed by Lightning Source
La Vergne, TN
USA

The paper is 20% recycled
fibers and meets national
standards of a recycled product.

www.myextraspecialsibling.com

Proceeds from the sale of this book will benefit children and families with fragile X syndrome. The Fragile X Association of Georgia is a nonprofit 501(c)(3) organization, and contributions are tax deductible.

To all the lucky kids out there who are blessed with a brother or sister with special needs.

Contents

Foreword: Why I Wrote This Book xi

Preface xiii

eXtra Special Acknowledgments xv

A Note To My Readers xvii

Carly's Ten Commandments For Being
    An eXtra Special Sibling xix

What Makes Scott So Special?   1

The Fragile X Talk   3

A Wake-Up Call   5

Embarrassing Moments   7

Love Him No Matter What 11

"Hi, My Name Is Scott" 13

Let's Go Waterskiing! 19

That "Special" Day 23

My Favorite Copycat Moment 25

Dancing The Night Away 29

Road Trip 33

That Special Radar 35

Celebrating The Little Things In Life 37

Graduation Day 39

Working Together 43

Words From Scott 45

Conclusion 47

ꙮ♥ꙮ eXtras ꙮ♥ꙮ

FAQ (Frequently Asked Questions) 49

    Does Scott look funny? 49

    Can Scott walk, or is he in a wheelchair? 49

    Will Scott ever be able to drive a car? 49

    Does Scott go to school? 49

    Does Scott have a girlfriend? Will he ever
       get married? 50

    What kind of support is Scott going to need
       as he gets older? 50

    Does Scott know he has fragile X? 51

    Do you ever think Scott gets more attention
       because he is special? 52

    Do you ever wonder what Scott would be like
       if he did not have fragile X? 52

    Do you ever wish Scott did not have fragile X? 53

Did You Know...? An Expert Answers Your Technical Fragile X Questions 55

What is fragile X syndrome? 55

What is a genetic disorder? 55

What are other genetic disorders? 55

What is a mental impairment? 56

How common is fragile X syndrome? 56

What is a carrier? 56

What is premutation? 57

What are the statistics about siblings? 57

What is the life expectancy for people who
    have fragile X syndrome? 58

Is there a cure for fragile X syndrome? 58

Can you "catch" fragile X syndrome? 58

What about other special needs? 58

Resources 59

Organizations That Work With Children
    With Special Needs 60

Sibling Support Web Sites For Families
    With Special Needs 62

Magazines Of Interest 62

Photo Gallery 63

Activity Worksheets 78

Foreword: Why I Wrote This Book

Carly Heyman

I never dreamed I would write a book, but through Scott I have been inspired to try to help others enjoy a closer relationship with their special brothers and sisters.

Living with a sibling with special needs is not always easy. In my case, I have had sixteen wonderful years of practice, and I like to think of myself as an expert fragile X sister. In this book, I share several personal "Scott stories"—some embarrassing, some emotional, some serious, and some just plain funny.

I hope these "Scott stories" will help trigger some memories of your own and allow you to see your relationship with your sibling in a more positive way than you might have done in the past. My goal is to help you feel more comfortable knowing there are other families out there going through similar experiences.

So—welcome to my world. I will tell you how I survive the rough times and celebrate the good times. I share real-life stories, including both the happy and the sad. I wrote this book to inspire you to love your brother or sister unconditionally because this special love helps both of you to grow.

I hope you will also see how growing up with a family member who has special needs prepares us for life's challenges. Learning to be accepting, understanding, and patient will make the rest of your life easier. If you can manage to add a sense of humor, you will have even more fun.

Your situation might be slightly different from mine, but boy oh boy, do we have a lot in common!

Preface

From the time our children were very young, Carly and her oldest brother, Jared, have been devoted siblings to Scott. They have loved him unconditionally, but like all young children, they have struggled with his differences. However, this book is about the journey from accepting his uniqueness to rejoicing in his individuality.

A high school teacher's assignment first prompted Carly to write about her experiences living with a brother with fragile X syndrome. While writing, she was sometimes exhilarated and at other times frustrated as she put so many thoughts into words—this was a very personal project for her. We encouraged it because we thought the book would help others. We—her parents—were not allowed to read the text until a month before it was published. Then, we laughed and we cried—and we celebrated the creation of this book as we reflected on what it means to be a family.

This book is a labor of pure love. However, it's not only about the love that a younger sister feels for her "eXtra special" brother—it is also about the feelings and the struggle of all young people who wrestle with issues surrounding their own acceptance, understanding, and love of their siblings.

We are immensely proud of our daughter. It is our hope that the message in this book will open doors between siblings so that the pride, the joy, and the love Carly shares with Scott will be an inspiration to you and your family.

Gail and Lyons Heyman
January 2003

eXtra Special Acknowledgments

First, I thank the star of the book—my big brother, Scott Henry Heyman. Scott is one of the coolest, most awesome people I know, and I would like to thank him for being himself. I definitely could not have written this book if it were not for him.

And I must not forget to thank my oldest brother, Jared, who has taught me so much about life. I admire him very much and see him as the greatest possible role model. Jared sets the tone of how siblings should love and respect each other, and I simply try to follow in his footsteps. As for the book, I know he is proud of me—after all, he teases me by saying he wants me to write a sequel called *Jared and Me*.

Of course, none of us would even be here if it were not for Mom and Dad. Our parents have always been loving, supportive, and understanding of all three of their children; they are truly extraordinary. I owe everything I am to my parents. They guide me through life in the most beautiful way, and I am grateful to them for making me who I am today. I am lucky to have two such eXtra special parents!

In addition to my nuclear family, I also thank my indescribably close extended family—I consider myself very fortunate to have such loving support. First, I thank my grandparents: Grandma Betty and Papa Leon and Nana and Poppy; next, my wonderful aunts and uncles: Aunt Liz and Uncle Bobby, Aunt Karen and Uncle Steven, Aunt Janet and Uncle Sam, Aunt Debbie and Uncle Scott, and Aunt Donna and Uncle David; and, of course, my fun-loving first cousins: Adam, Mindy, Sherri, Jeffery, Blair, Alan, Todd, Michael, Laura, and Lindsay.

Our good friend Stephanie Conley has contributed immeasurably to this book. Ever since she and I played softball together as kids, we have shared a special, close relationship. Recalling some of our fun memories, she has beautifully illustrated this book. Thank you, Stephanie, for everything!

I also thank my friends—old and new—who inspired me and helped me write this book: my eleventh-grade English teacher, Mrs. Lee, for assigning her students to write a paper on genetics, which in turn encouraged me to write this book about Scott; Robyn Spizman, for being my absolute number one motivator and mentor and whose positive attitude and encouragement have guided the writing of this book; and Evie Sacks, Linda Frysh, Jeffery Cohen, Dr. Vickie Fedele, Karen Shelnutt, Ava Wilensky, and Candance Paetzhold for the hours they spent reviewing the manuscript.

In addition, I thank my two best friends, Rachel and Matt, for always being available to listen and support me, not only throughout this book but also throughout my entire life. Our friendship is outstanding, and I cherish it and you.

I also thank Dr. Stephanie Sherman and Stephen Warren for their research at the Department of Medical Genetics at Emory University; Robby Miller of the National Fragile X Foundation; Katie Clapp of FRAXA Research Foundation; Jerrie Paschal of ARC Cobb (Association of Retarded Citizens); and CeCe Pressly of Special Olympics Georgia.

Also, this book would not have been possible without the indispensable technical assistance and direction of Julia Houk of Lightning Source; Martha Nichols of aMuse Productions; our wonderful cover photographer, Warren Bond; and Jeff Davis of WSB Radio for helping me produce this book on tape.

There is not room to list the names of the many teachers, coaches, friends, and family members to whom I owe a great debt of gratitude for the guidance and love they have provided me during the first seventeen years of my life. You know who you are, and I truly appreciate everything you do for me.

A Note To My Readers

My name is Carly, and I have an eXtra-special brother named Scott. I am related to Scott by blood—but we are best friends by choice. I am Scott's fashion and dressing consultant, motivator, mentor, listener, and most of all, his biggest fan.

I see my brother as a little gift from God. Yes, living with Scott's special needs is difficult at times, but Scott enriches my life in ways that no one else ever could.

Having a sibling with special needs is a huge responsibility, but if you keep a positive attitude and a great sense of humor, the responsibilities can turn into some of life's greatest pleasures. Anyone living with a brother or sister with special needs knows that life can be challenging at times, but I would like to show you how it can also be a joy. Our siblings have so much to offer, and it is up to us to recognize the many good things they bring to the relationship. Loving them and spending time with them is more than fun—it can teach us some very important lessons.

I feel lucky to have grown up with such a special older brother, and I hope to open your eyes so you can see how lucky you are, too.

Carly's
Ten Commandments
For Being An
eXtra Special Sibling

1. Be understanding of your sibling's special needs.

2. Take time to bond with your brother or sister.

3. Enjoy the easy moments and learn from the difficult ones.

4. Try to forget the embarrassing incidents and move on.

5. Stay optimistic and celebrate the little things in life.

6. Accept your sibling's strengths and weaknesses.

7. Do not be afraid to challenge your sibling.

8. Encourage your sibling to be friends with your friends.

9. Be available to help your parents whenever possible.

10. Most importantly, show your sibling how much you love him or her!

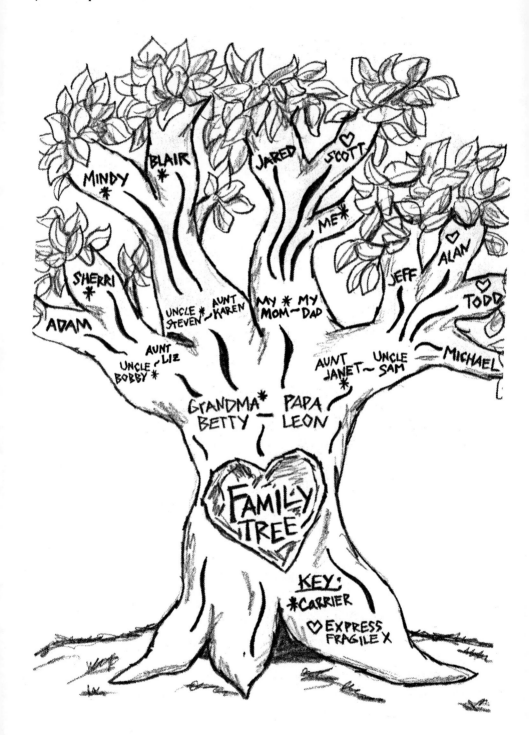

What Makes Scott So Special?

Scott was diagnosed with fragile X syndrome in 1989, during a time when scientists were still exploring the gene that causes this disorder. I was four years old, and Scott was nine. No one in my family had ever heard of fragile X, and we were unfamiliar with developmental disabilities in general, so this discovery came as quite a shock. However, my parents, extended family, and friends already knew something was different about Scott. He was hyperactive, made strange noises, and had a hard time communicating.

My parents were concerned and searched for answers, but nothing seemed to make sense. At one point, they thought Scott was deaf because they could never get his attention. They had his hearing tested but found nothing wrong.

After nine frustrating years, my parents finally got some answers. Doctors diagnosed Scott with fragile X syndrome, an inherited cause of mental retardation that would alter his life—and ours— forever.

Soon after Scott was diagnosed, my family members and I were also tested for fragile X. Doctors traced this special gene to my maternal grandmother. (I want to emphasize that it wasn't her "fault" that she carried the gene—it had come down through countless generations before her.) The doctors explained that she had passed fragile X chromosome to her four children and, through them, to seven of her grandchildren. Three of her grandsons express the gene, meaning that they physically and mentally "show" fragile X syndrome; all four of her granddaughters are *carriers* of the gene, meaning we carry the gene but do not show any symptoms of the disorder.

The Fragile X Talk

When I was about four years old, my parents told me that Scott had a mental impairment called fragile X syndrome. At that tender age, I probably just thought, "Okay, whatever...! So, what's for dinner?" I accepted what my parents told me but didn't really understand. I knew Scott had something wrong with him, but it was no big deal.

However, as I got older, I started to notice how Scott was different from other kids. His hyperactivity and disturbing behavior made him very difficult to manage and definitely made him stand out in a crowd. I was often embarrassed when he made public scenes. Although I was angry, I tried to remember my parent's words: "Scott cannot always control the way he acts, and you should love him no matter what."

I admit it was hard for me to understand these concepts of acceptance and patience. However, through living with Scott and learning from my parents' positive attitude, I feel I have become a better person. I have learned these life lessons from many sources, but of all people, Scott has been my best teacher.

Looking back, I appreciate the fact that I was told about Scott's disabilities when I was very young. My family never seemed embarrassed or ashamed of his impairment—instead, they made fragile X seem like the coolest thing ever. My parents told me in a way that was serious, yet positive. Calmly and naturally, they let me know Scott was different from most kids but that he was still my big brother. Although I was first introduced to the concept of fragile X as a preschooler, only recently have I realized its true significance and how it has affected my life.

A Wake-Up Call

Learning to read is a big event in the life of any child, so it was a wake-up call for me when I first realized that Scott, my older brother, could not read. I knew Scott was mentally impaired, but I still thought he could learn to read. I clearly remember approaching my mom and dad and telling them how they needed to take more time to teach Scott. My parents simply explained that he was unable to read because his brain did not work that way. My oldest brother Jared could read, so I wondered, "Why can't Scott read?" and I took it upon myself to teach him. How hard could it really be?

I soon found out! After many lessons, we had made absolutely no progress. Scott would get frustrated, then I would get frustrated, and then Scott would run away.

Perhaps the source of my enthusiasm for teaching Scott to read was my need for him to be a normal kid. In most families it is the older siblings who are more advanced—why couldn't it be like that in my family, too? At that naïve age, I was unwilling to accept Scott's limitations. Acknowledging shortcomings in someone you love is difficult, but it is an important skill to develop. It would not have been fair to Scott—or to me—if I had continued to pressure him to learn to read.

Scott taught me the importance of accepting others' weaknesses. Scott and I have now turned reading into an activity during which we can just enjoy each other's company. I read Scott

It is important to acknowledge your sibling's shortcomings

menus, magazines, and letters he gets in the mail. I take it as a compliment that Scott comes to me more often than anyone else to have something read. (My brother Jared may argue with this, but that is just because he is jealous that I have been chosen for this honor!)

Although Scott can't pick up a teen magazine and read the latest news, he can now identify familiar words from having seen them over and over again. I like to interpret Scott's selection of words as a representation of his priorities in life. For example, Scott can recognize words such as "Carly," "Texas" (where Jared went to college), or "Wheeler"—his much-loved high school. Whenever I see Scott "reading," I let him know how proud I am of him, and each time I am rewarded with that beautiful smile of his that always brightens my day!

Embarrassing Moments

There were many embarrassing moments for me when Scott and I were younger. A typical site for these events was the grocery store. Sometimes my mom and I would be preoccupied and accidentally wander off to another aisle and forget to tell Scott where we were headed. When Scott realized we were not by his side, he would throw a fit, screaming and crying because he could not find us. I couldn't blame him for feeling scared, but it was difficult to deal with his inappropriate behavior. The other customers would look at him strangely— they didn't understand why a fifteen-year-old boy was having a temper tantrum.

This was tough on me. I hated it when people stared at Scott even though I knew they didn't mean anything by it. At times like these, I wished people knew he had fragile X syndrome—a legitimate reason for his behavior. I wanted to explain why he was acting like a baby, but I couldn't. I realized these people probably did not even care why Scott was acting weird. He was just different, so they stared.

When my mom would say we were going to the grocery store or some other public place, I would sometimes shiver with dread, anticipating a possible scene.

I remember many times I left the house happy and ready for an innocent outing to buy groceries, then returned embarrassed and ashamed because my older brother had cried in the middle of the cereal aisle. I am not proud of that feeling, but I guess it was just part of growing up with

Learn how to handle your sibling's comfort zones & limits

a brother with special needs. I was ten, and I knew how to act in public. Scott, on the other hand, was fifteen, but he acted like he was five. It was a tough problem for a little kid like me to figure out, and I did what I could, but it did not always turn out to be such a great job.

As I've gotten older, I've learned more about Scott's comfort zones and limitations and how to handle them. If the grocery store situation sounds familiar, then perhaps you might benefit from my experiences. I have learned that Scott does not like to leave the house for long periods of time. He usually gets bored, anxious, and then frustrated, which in turn causes him to throw a temper tantrum. Having seen this happen many times, I have come to realize Scott does better on shorter trips. Instead of going to the grocery store for about an hour, my mom and I learned to take him on quicker runs, like to the gas station to pick up some milk.

Teaching our siblings to leave the house—which is their comfort zone— is an essential part of their becoming more comfortable in public situations.

Time	Scott
30 min.	☺
1 hr. 30 min.	😐
2 hr. 30 min.	☹
3 hr. 30 min.	😫

Getting out and experiencing the world is a fun part of life I would hate to have our siblings miss. So when you are away from home, try to make sure your brother or sister is always nearby. Our siblings get very distracted, and it would be horrible to lose your buddy.

I have also realized the more we take Scott out, the easier it is for him to leave the house. It was always a hassle to pull him away from the TV set, but the more we encouraged him to leave, the more confident he became. I know you may be thinking that some of these concerns are your parents' responsibility, but since we are closer to our siblings in age, I believe we can often be more effective at guiding them through these everyday challenges.

Encourage your sibling & they will become more confident.

Another great way to help your family member venture out from the house is to invite them to one of your own activities. For example, I play fast-pitch softball and everyone—including me—loves it when Scott comes to watch my games. It is good not only for Scott to get outside and socialize, but also for me to have the opportunity to enjoy his company.

Scott is by far my high school's number one ball-boy. Scott runs to get those foul balls faster than anyone else I have seen. I love having my brother, my number one fan, come to my games. Whenever I am up at bat, I hear him yelling, "Let's go, Boo!" (my nickname). Hearing Scott's boisterous and enthusiastic voice from the stands makes me the happiest player on the field.

Love Him No Matter What

The motto in our family is "Love him no matter what." There are plenty of times when Scott embarrasses me or prevents me from participating in various activities, but I will continue to love him no matter what. Even when the family can't go snow skiing because Scott doesn't like cold weather, we continue to love him. Even though he can't read, or remember to shave, or count to twenty, or drive a car, or take down phone messages, he is still my big brother, and I will always love him.

In other words, even if your brother or sister embarrasses you in public or in front of your friends, love him or her no matter what. If your sibling throws a temper tantrum, take a deep breath and try to get over it! We all have our moments. It will only last a few minutes, and there are more important things in life. Instead, focus more on the happier times you have shared. I know how it feels to get unwanted stares from people who don't understand, but that is a small price to pay for having such eXtra special siblings.

Also, I have noticed that the calmer I am with my brother when he acts up, the better the result. Freaking out or trying to hide or shame your sibling in this type of situation is never good. Your sibling gets upset, you get embarrassed, and the scene simply gets bigger. We all act a little weird or out of control sometimes—it's okay; move on.

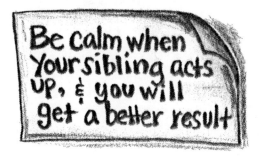

"Hi, My Name Is Scott"

"Hi, my name is Scott."

It sounds like such a simple phrase, but for Scott it's not so easy. But why can't he just say it? Why can't Scott just look someone in the eye and introduce himself properly?

Introducing Scott to new friends has always been an interesting part of my life. I will tell you how I have handled my "Scott introductions" from beginning to end, and I hope it is helpful to you.

When I was about seven years old, I did not even bother trying to give my friends a heads-up to the fact that my brother is unique. I always just went for it and said like any other kid, "Yeah, and this is my big brother, Scott." For most siblings that would be it—done; no more questions. However, with Scott, it was a much bigger challenge.

I can clearly remember many times walking home from school with a new friend and finding Scott doing something odd, like talking to himself while playing basketball outside. I wouldn't think twice about this behavior, but my new friend would become uncomfortable, give my brother a funny look, and then turn to me for some answers.

I would feel responsible for my friend's feelings and would try to explain my brother's behavior. I didn't want to scare my friends away or have them think that *I* was not normal just because my *brother* was not exactly normal.

After that awkward first impression, I would begin my typical speech: "Yeah, my brother is a little different; he has something called fragile X syndrome." Most often the response would be, "Okay, but what does that mean?"

Even though I had grown up with him, I barely understood the term *fragile X*. How could I expect another seven-year-old to understand this complicated syndrome?

I often tried to explain further by saying, "Fragile X is a type of mental impairment," and when this didn't work, I said that his brain worked differently, that he was born with this syndrome, and that because of it he acted a lot younger than he was.

There was always so much to explain, and at that age all I wanted to do was play. But I felt it was my responsibility to give my friends a reasonable answer they would understand.

Later, around age eleven, I realized it was better to explain Scott's disability before people actually met him. Some friends knew other kids who had special needs, but most did not. It was always easier on me when a friend knew a little bit about people with special needs, but if they didn't, that only meant I had to be more patient. Sometimes my friends would share a story about someone they knew with special needs, but usually the disorders they described were totally different from fragile X. Trust me, I've heard about some pretty extreme but unrelated conditions.

With my friends who were totally unfamiliar with mental impairments, I would have to start from the beginning. After my standard explanation, the questions would begin. Can he talk? Can he read? Can he walk? I don't know how many times I have answered the same questions, but as I get older, I am more patient and more willing to explain. The more open I am to sharing and answering these questions, the better the result. If I am enthusiastic and positive—and comfortable— when answering, my friends also become more comfortable. However, I will caution you that around middle school, kids tend to become more judgmental and less willing to accept different kinds of people. Trust yourself— and choose your friends wisely.

Although I've grown to enjoy introducing Scott to friends, there were many times when I wished he were normal so he could do it himself. Life would have been so much easier, but, hey—that's what makes it fun, right? It was difficult at times, but I never let it stop me from inviting friends over. Now, at age sixteen, I find it a joy to introduce Scott to my friends. I start it off with the typical: Scott…fragile X…special needs…mental impairment…etc.

Fortunately, by the time they reach my age, most people are already familiar with the special needs vocabulary.

The rest of the conversation is usually determined by my friend's reaction. If they respond with "No problem," then we move on. However, if they start asking questions, then the "Scott introduction" speech continues: Yes, he can talk; no, he cannot read; he has the academic capability of a third grader; no, he is not in a wheelchair; he is not physically impaired at all; and he looks like most other kids. Then I allow for a little pause to see if there are any more questions—and usually there are.

Questions

1. Can Scott read?

2. What is Fragile X Syndrome?

3. Does Scott make weird noises?

4. Can Scott talk or understand our conversation?

5. How is Scott different or special?

What exactly makes him so different? I personally find this question the most difficult one to answer. I love him so much that sometimes I simply don't want to talk about his weaknesses. As a joke, I sometimes want to say, "Stick around, you'll see...!" but instead I explain that he does unexpected weird things, cannot carry on a full conversation, and cannot express his feelings clearly.

That's usually enough, but with my more science-oriented friends, the questions continue. Where did this come from? I answer to the best of my ability and smile. I try to be patient and find the satisfaction in educating my friends about a subject with which they are unfamiliar but in which *I* am an expert.

I find that my attitude towards Scott greatly influences the way my friends interact with him. I set the example. If I were embarrassed or ashamed of Scott, my new friend would immediately have a negative opinion of him. However, if I act like he is the coolest kid—which he is—my friends are more willing to develop their own silly jokes with him. It makes me feel good inside to see my brother socialize with my friends. But if friends, for whatever the reason, do not connect with Scott right away, that is also okay. I have found that the more time they spend in the Heyman household, the more they are going to warm up to Scott and want to be his friend.

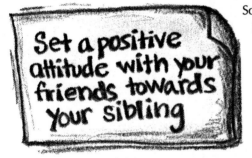

Set a positive attitude with your friends towards your sibling

When I finally complete my "Scott introductions," I *always* tell my friends how cool Scott really is. I say he is a great guy and an awesome and fun person to be around. I let them know how he likes playing repetitive little games with people and how it never gets old for him. I encourage them, for example, to create their own nicknames for Scott so he will love them forever. Some silly nicknames have developed over the years, including "Buster," "Uncle Scott," "Bubba," or even the greatest: "Meathead!" I usually end the introduction with these nicknames to finish on a happy note.

Let's Go Waterskiing!

I vividly remember one of my proudest "Scott moments." It was a typical early summer morning at the family vacation house at Lake Lanier. Waterskiing has always been one of my family's favorite activities. I learned to water ski when I was seven, and I've grown up watching my brother Jared ski, but for Scott, it was a little different. Scott had tried to ski during the past several years without success. Little did I know this particular Sunday morning would prove to be such a proud moment.

It was about 8:00 A.M. The water was as smooth as glass, and the temperature was just right. I was sitting in the stern of the boat, my dad was in the driver's seat, and Scott was in the water holding tightly onto the rope. As always, once he was ready to try to get up, Scott cried out, "Hit it, Dad!" The engine roared. Scott popped right out of the water as if he had been skiing all his life. He knew he was "da man!" as he finally stayed up on two skis. That was one of the greatest mornings ever.

The huge smile on Scott's face showed his happiness and pride in this incredible accomplishment. You see, my family is very physically active, and we enjoy such adventurous sports as rock-climbing, hiking, and biking. I always knew Scott could participate in these activities, but I honestly did not think he would ever be able to ski. Watching him rise out of the water and seeing that grin take over his face left me with a warm feeling I will never forget. My dad never seemed to have a doubt, though, and encouraged Scott all the way. (Or if he was doubtful, he did not *show* it, which is a pretty good lesson for a parent of any child trying something new.) I often like to revisit

Show your sibling how proud you are of their accomplishments!

that picture in my mind so I can remember how proud I felt of my big brother. Those hours of encouragement in the water really paid off.

Recently, we were at the lake and Scott got the chance to show off his waterskiing skills to my friends. They were very impressed. I was glowing with pride, and Scott was shining like a superstar. Now, here's a fact—there ain't nuttin' better than a happy Scott!

The truth is, Scott constantly surprises us with his abilities. So remember: Never give up on your sibling with special needs and never underestimate his or her abilities. We all know their needs are different, but that does not mean we can't push them to succeed. Positive encouragement and optimism are good ways to motivate Scott—and anyone else for that matter.

But encouraging a sibling with special needs is not always as easy as it might sound. These kids are not always able to tell you how far you can push, and pushing too far is not a good idea. So keep in mind that an unhappy sibling is not worth a new skill.

Developing a close relationship with your brother or sister and spending time with them can help you to better understand their strengths and weaknesses. When it came to Scott and waterskiing, this was the family strategy: We knew Scott was physically strong and athletic and liked the water—all helpful qualities. However, we also knew that he was not very

patient about practicing things over and over again, so it generally takes him a long time to learn something new. Because of this knowledge, we had a lot of short practice sessions, and we worked on the skiing slowly over two whole summers.

When you spend time together you build a bond, which, in turn, builds trust. Therefore, the process (in our case, it involved learning to water ski) can be nearly as much fun as the end result (being able to ski). Once you know your sibling's limits and have their trust, then sit back, relax, and watch them thrive.

Spend time together to develop a bond of trust & understanding

That "Special" Day

"Let me win, but if I cannot win, let me be brave
in the attempt."

Special Olympics Athlete Oath

It was the morning of the big powerlifting event in the Special Olympics Georgia Winter Games, and I can still remember sitting on the floor of that hot, sweaty-smelling gym with all my friends and family around me as we watched my big brother with amazement. For an entire year, Scott had worked with his Special Olympics coach and buddy, Harry. The big day had finally arrived. Scott was so happy and proud of himself and knew everyone was there to support him.

Scott felt that support as he lifted weights heavier than his own body weight. As he grunted and held that bar, his eyes filled with determination—he knew he could do it, and he did! I was incredibly proud. We all were. To this day, it is one of my greatest feelings to be able to share my pride in Scott's Special Olympics successes with family and friends.

Whenever someone asks how the family is doing, we tell them about Scott's accomplishments in Special Olympics powerlifting, golf and basketball, and the listener is always blown away. Jared and I love to sit back and let Scott take the spotlight. Over five years, he won eleven gold medals in powerlifting and another gold medal in golf and one for basketball—pretty amazing, huh? Scott proudly hangs all thirteen of his gold medals in his room for everyone to see and admire.

My older brother Jared and I had always participated in sports, and Scott had always been there to cheer us on. Now, it was finally his turn, and the fact that we were there to cheer for *him* was so very important.

There may not be many activities your sibling can participate in, so when they find their niche or passion, support them in every way possible. Share

Invite them
to one of
Your activities

with them how great you think it is that they have a particular interest or ability.

Being involved in such organizations as the Special Olympics year-round or simply having interesting hobbies helps our siblings socialize and stay active. They may not have the same medal-winning experience Scott did with Special Olympics, but be sure to praise each accomplishment, even if it is just winning a game of checkers with a family member or bowling a great game. Our siblings' successes can best be seen with an open mind and a loving heart.

My Favorite Copycat Moment

I remember how frustrated I was when I realized that Scott did not know how to read. I knew Scott was physically ten years old, but I did not understand that he was mentally stuck at about age five. It is important to recognize the ability level of your sibling and accept it rather than trying to change reality. Being patient and accepting is a very effective way to make your brother or sister feel comfortable rather than stupid. Let your siblings know that you understand them and love them no matter what they can or cannot do. Tell your brother or sister they are the coolest, smartest, or most handsome person in the world.

Tell your sibling you don't care about what they can & cannot do – you still love them

Sometimes it is difficult to see that Scott is maturing—it happens so slowly. Do not *ever* give up on your brothers or sisters or think they will never "grow up." They will and they do; it's just delayed. For example, when Scott was younger, it did not seem to me that he cared about anything because he did not express his feelings very well. However, as Scott has grown older, he has learned to show clearly his love for his dog, his school, and, of course, his favorite wrestling show on TV.

Sometimes, signs of maturity show up in the most unexpected places. When our cousin Neal graduated from high school, we attended a graduation party in his honor. It was a typical party with lots of food, drink, and people— things were going swell.

Don't think your sibling will never "grow up"

As we were preparing to leave, I quickly signed the guest book by the door. I wrote,

Neal,
  Congratulations! It is so cool that you
  are going to college now, can't wait to visit you!
    - cousin Carly

When I finished writing, I passed the pen to the person next to me, not paying attention to who it was. It turned out to be Scott! Now, Scott can't really read or write, so why would he have been waiting for that pen? But before we left, Scott tapped me on the shoulder and pointed to the guest book with a big smile. In Scott's first grade handwriting, I saw,

Neal Congratulations It issacool that you

are goignto coLeg e now Can't watto visit you!

Causin scott Heyman

Seeing this sentence warmed my heart. This simple sentence may not mean a lot to most people, but it meant everything to me. It expressed Scott's love, intelligence, trust, and maturity. Scott copied that sentence for many reasons. First, he wanted to communicate his love and show his pride in his cousin's accomplishment. Second, Scott wanted to participate in this celebration just like the rest of us. No one told Scott to write anything. He was smart enough to know that this was a way he could express his congratulations. Scott trusted that whatever I had written would be appropriate for him, too. Most importantly, this sentence represented Scott's progress. Rather than not participating, he found his own way to express himself. When he pointed to the guest book with that accomplished smile on his face, he knew he had done something really amazing, and I was so glad I was there to share it with him.

I got a great deal of joy out of that one copycat moment. To most people, this sentence would have looked unoriginal, but to me it looked fantastic because it showed my brother's development.

Dancing The Night Away

Because Scott was able to stay in school until he was twenty-one, he had three years as a senior, each very special to him. During Scott's "second senior year," he, like most other students, wanted to attend his high school prom. He knew what was going on around him, and he wanted to be part of it in every way.

As my parents were making the plans, I overheard my mom on the phone saying how she was a little concerned that Scott and his friends with special needs might feel intimidated or overwhelmed when they arrived at the party. So, devoted little sister that I am, I volunteered to go with Scott and his friends to the prom. I also brought one of my good friends who is close to Scott and his group. At times like this, it is better for you to accompany your sibling than for your parents to do so. I do not know any parents who have attended their teenager's high school prom.

I thought it would be pretty cool for a freshman like me to go to a junior/ senior prom and, more importantly, I did not want Scott to feel intimidated. I asked Scott if he would mind if I went with him, and he simply nodded and gave a sigh of relief.

Prom night rolled around, and after the huge picture party at our house, the limousine came to pick up us kids. I thought I would have to keep a close eye on Scott and his friends to make sure they were happy and comfortable. I assumed the other students at the prom would ignore these boys and continue dancing. I had seen Scott socialize with the other teens at his school at various basketball and football games, and because he was manager of the girl's varsity basketball team for four years, I had always seen the Wheeler

Know that Others love your sibling too!

students being nice to Scott and smiling at him. But I thought this was the extent of their relationship with him.

It was not until I saw the genuine excitement in the other students' eyes when Scott took to the dance floor that I realized how much these kids really did love him. Scott was shining that night, not only in my eyes but also in the eyes of his entire senior class. It was the coolest feeling to realize that I was not the only one enjoying his company. I wanted everyone to know I was Scott's little sister. Although he might not have been able to read as well as most high school kids, he could still dance with the best of them!

Scott enjoys and admires his school friends very much, but there is also a warm place in his heart for his "special" friends. Scott loves to hang out and

play sports with these other friends, including Russell and Paul. These three guys are very close and very active. They like to go bowling, play basketball, hit golf balls, watch TV, or just chill around the house, like all teenage boys. Scott, Russell, and Paul may not have the most philosophical conversations, but they still share an amazing friendship.

It is a joy to watch Scott interact with both his typical and his special friends. He loves and appreciates both groups very much even though they socialize in different ways. Your sibling may also relate to different types of friends, or they may prefer one to the other. Whichever the case, encourage them to socialize with people their age; it makes life more fun.

In addition to Russell and Paul, Scott has two other close companions with special needs, Alan and Todd, who also happen to be our first cousins. The rest of the cousins and I love spending time with these three boys, and we all get along royally. It is great to have family support, and Scott and I both know its importance. There is nothing like a family reunion with three eXtra special boys!

Road Trip

As you know, having a sibling with special needs can be a lot of fun. I love spending my free time with Scott, and he somehow entertains me by having me do some of the most ridiculous things. I often find myself laughing with Scott more than anyone else.

One day I was driving Scott and Russell to the University of Georgia in Athens for a dance with their friends. During the hour-and-a-half drive, I was starting to get bored and needed some sort of entertainment. Scott picked up on my boredom and decided it would be fun to lower the windows and shout every time we drove by a sign that read "Athens." Well, the closer we got to Athens, the louder and windier the car became. It was a silly game, but because the boys like routines and repetition, nobody got sick of it.

That was just one of the many special memories I share with Scott. I've learned that it's the simplest games that can turn into the most enjoyable bonding experiences. One of the greatest joys of hanging out with Scott is that I can be my silliest self—something I treasure and hope I will never lose.

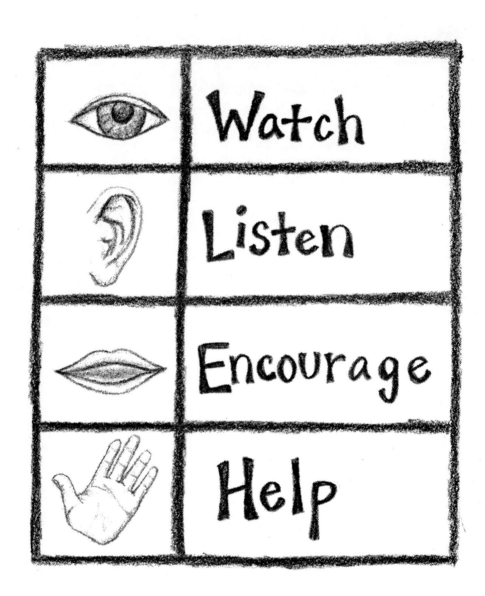

Watch

Listen

Encourage

Help

That Special Radar

Often, people are confused about who is older—Scott or me. It can be difficult or embarrassing to be the physically younger but intellectually more mature sibling. In my case, I am the baby of the family *and* the only daughter—a position I have grown to love. After all, I have two big brothers looking after me and giving me all sorts of attention. However, there are also many times when my special radar tells me that I need to take on the role of the older sibling and take care of Scott in a variety of ways.

People with special needs are "stuck" at different ages in different aspects of their life. For example, Scott is simultaneously twenty-one years old physically, eight years old academically, and around twelve years old socially. Ouch! That may sound a little harsh, or even too direct, but that's the way it is, and it helps me to keep that in mind.

This age conflict comes up in various places, such as at restaurants. If I sit next to Scott when we go out to dinner, I know it is my responsibility to help him order. I also know that Scott sometimes gets embarrassed because he cannot understand the menu, so I will either read the menu to him or just read it out loud, kind of to myself. This makes him feel comfortable, as well as smart, which he is. I try to recognize, accept, and love all Scott's different ages, even when it is not convenient for me.

Accept your sibling's "functional ages"

As siblings of individuals with special needs, we need to accept our brothers' or sisters' functional ages and realize that we are among the very few people who can really understand these age discrepancies. Instead of getting frustrated when they don't "act their age," let your siblings know through your kind actions that you are willing to help them. Be aware of their needs and have your special radar up as often as possible—this is the secret to success. And this is also very important: eXtra special siblings *need to have* eXtra special siblings!

Celebrating The Little Things In Life

There are many things in my life that I am able to do that Scott is not. Reading, driving, and scuba diving are three that come to mind. However, there are other things Scott has accomplished that I haven't, and that makes me proud. For example, Scott's first real job was working on staff at Camp Barney Medintz, an overnight summer camp in northern Georgia. For

years, Scott has worked hard in the dining hall there—taking out the trash, wiping down the tables, and helping prepare the meals for the entire camp. These tasks are difficult for him, but Scott carries them out beautifully. I did not think he would be able to sustain a job, but Scott has proven to me, to himself, and also to his family and friends what a reliable and efficient worker he has become.

I look up to Scott and respect him immensely for becoming a successful worker and a more independent person. This has taught me it's a good idea to challenge your siblings to try activities they would not normally attempt. In

our household, Scott's successes in the camp dining hall are celebrated with the same amount of enthusiasm as if he had been elected President of the United States! Although he may have fewer accomplishments than most, as a family we make it a priority to celebrate each and every one of Scott's achievements.

Even if your sibling may only do things that seem trivial or unimpressive to others, don't let that discourage you from seeing their accomplishments as major life events—because that's what they are. I know that some people might not think working as a member of a camp staff cleaning tables and taking out the trash is such a big deal, but to me, it is huge. When Scott achieves something that I have yet to experience, I make sure he knows how impressed and proud I am.

Graduation Day

Saturday, May 25: Wow! I will never forget that day—Scott Heyman's high school graduation. Congratulations! Having completed seven awesome years at Wheeler High School, Scott deserved a big celebration, and that is exactly what he got.

Scott had the ideal high school experience. Every morning he got himself ready, walked to the bus stop, went to the same familiar class, learned with and from the same familiar faces, socialized with his caring classmates, and returned to his comfortable home. Scott's school days were very predictable and orderly, exactly the way he likes things.

Wheeler High School meant the world to him, and words can't express its importance. So graduation was a red-letter day on our family's calendar, an occasion we will never forget. Scott will not graduate from college and will probably not get married and have children like most people we know. So it is important that we as a family recognize all Scott's major events, like graduation, in a big way.

Immediately following Commencement, we had a huge celebration at our house. Only Scott's nearest and dearest—100 people!— were invited, and nearly every one of them showed up.

At one point during the party, I was talking with some of our guests and realized everyone was looking for me

because Scott wanted me to come out to the backyard.

I headed to the deck to see what was up. There he was, the graduation boy, chilling on a lawn chair with his closest buddies surrounding him. It was a gorgeous sight to see—Scott, glowing with pride. He asked me to bring him a cup of water from the kitchen, but it was clear that the water was not really what Scott wanted. He just wanted me to be near him and to show me how proud he was of himself.

Scott has special ways of communicating his feelings, and by being a close little sister I am usually able to detect what he really wants. I know Scott would never actually say, "Carly, come celebrate this spectacular night with me," but by calling me over from the other side of the house, that is exactly what he communicated. So, I interpreted his simple request, got the cup of water, and chilled with him and his buddies until he was ready to move on. Maybe it was the fact that we've shared the same bathroom all our lives or maybe it was just sisterly intuition, but this incident made me realize how special our sibling connection really is.

Of course, all siblings have some sort of natural bond. Being closely tied into someone else's life creates an extra level of trust and understanding that is a special gift. I urge you to develop that natural bond and bring yourself even closer to your sibling. The tighter you become at an earlier age, the more likely you will be able to support each other in the future.

The "get the cup" incident certainly speaks to the strong connection between Scott and me. But if I had gotten annoyed with him for dragging me across the house for no apparent reason, I would have lost out on that bonding opportunity. With a negative outlook I could have interpreted his request as just a silly demand, but, instead, I responded based on my intuitive understanding of Scott. Because he is not able to express his feelings as clearly as others, I have had to learn to "read" my brother and interpret his feelings.

Think twice about responding in an annoyed or negative way to your siblings' strange gestures or requests. Keep a positive attitude and understand that they have fewer resources than you for communicating. As siblings, we should always be available for them. Our special brothers and sisters often look

to us for the trust and support that is so important to their comfort and happiness. Scott was a star that evening and he knew it. He shines in my eyes every day, but on Graduation Night, he was a superstar in front of all his friends and family.

During the days after the big event, I found myself thinking about what Scott's graduation represented to him and comparing that to what it meant to me. For Scott, graduation probably just meant a big party and perhaps the fear of having to change his routine. I don't think he understands his future or the implications of today's actions on the future.

For me, Scott's graduation represented one of his most important accomplishments and a vital step in his becoming more independent. However, Scott will never be totally independent, so I will have to support him in every way—much more than an average sibling. Although I've probably thought about this in the past, it has become clearer to me in recent months. I know I do not totally understand my responsibility to Scott yet, but at least now I am more aware of it. And because I love Scott so much, I am more than willing to be there for him—all the way.

Working Together

Scott has graduated from Wheeler High School. What now? Unlike my brother Jared and me—and nearly all the kids we know—Scott will not be going to college. Yikes! But my family has thought long and hard about other positive life options for Scott.

Because Scott is not able to tell us exactly how he feels or what he likes or dislikes, it's hard to plan his next steps. My mom, Dad, Jared, and I, along with our extended family and friends, must now work together to try to create a life for Scott that he will love. Fortunately, I am now old enough to be involved in the process. As a close sibling, I feel that I have a big responsibility to help Scott be happy. As a best friend, I want his future to be perfect; however, I know expecting to live a perfect life is not realistic for any of us.

I admit I have found myself thinking how much easier it would be if Scott were a typical kid planning his transition to college like my oldest brother, Jared, did seven years ago. But that's okay; it's just the way things are. As in earlier challenges with Scott, maintaining an optimistic attitude has helped me face this newest hurdle. We siblings may have to sacrifice our time or change priorities to help our brothers or sisters, but trust me—it's worth it in the end.

Words From Scott

As I was finishing this book, I decided to ask Scott if there was anything he wished to include. He obviously knew I was writing a book because of all the hours I have spent in front of this computer, so Scott and I talked, and he shared some of his ideas.

The first point Scott made was that he wants to make sure everyone is nice to his or her family. He knows the importance of supportive family members, and he knows we love him very much.

Next, Scott wants to encourage people with special needs to leave the house every now and then. He suggests people "go to football games or basketball games because they are fun." I guess all those hours of persuading him to get out have really paid off.

Scott also wants me to mention how hard he works at his job and how he helps his grandfather fix things around the lake house. Work is obviously on his mind at this time in his life, and he is proud of himself for what he has accomplished. To me, that shows he is grasping important life lessons. In fact, he was recently hired for his first full-time job!

Scott made another interesting statement: "Whenever someone dies, you have to know that they will always be in your heart." Later, I realized this is the same advice our father gives all his children when someone close passes away. Scott's statement showed that he really is listening and feeling and struggling with difficult concepts, and your sibling with special needs will be, too. Don't forget to share these struggles with them—you can help them and they can help you through whatever problems may arise in the future.

Conclusion

I am proud you took the time to read this book. It's an important first step toward becoming a super sibling. I hope my stories and advice have inspired you to explore your own relationship with your brother or sister with special needs. Much of what I have suggested is easier said than done, but it is certainly possible if you have a positive outlook. Remember, every individual is different, and there really is no right or wrong way to be a great sibling. Simply follow your heart and don't be afraid to show your love to your special brother or sister.

I am fortunate to have Scott as my brother. He has shaped my life by helping me become a more patient, accepting, understanding, open-minded, and loving person. I will cherish the contributions he has made to my life forever. I hope you can see the wonderful gifts our siblings bring into our lives.

Finally, and most importantly, I appreciate Scott just for being himself. If it were not for him, I would never have had the opportunity to write this book. I love my brother Scott very much, and I hope you see the light our siblings shine on us every day.

FAQ
(Frequently Asked Questions)

Does Scott look "funny"?

No, Scott does not look funny. Children with fragile X syndrome often have distinct physical characteristics, such as a long face and protruding ears. Personally, I think Scott is handsome and looks just like the rest of the family.

Can Scott walk, or is he in a wheelchair?

Yes, Scott can walk; he can even run, too. Scott is not physically disabled; in fact, his weight training has made him much stronger than either of his two siblings. Fragile X is a mental impairment, not a physical one.

Will Scott ever be able to drive a car?

No, Scott will never be able to drive a car. Scott is too impaired to make the many instant decisions required for driving on the road. Judgments that may seem routine to normal people can be life or death decisions for people with special needs. I think I would rather have Scott ride in my passenger seat—where he is very content—while I drive.

Does Scott go to school?

Yes, Scott graduated from our public high school, where there is a special education program. Scott attended special education classes for academics and regular education classes for art, P.E., home ec, horticulture, and mass-media productions. Scott was always happy in his classes and really enjoyed going to a school with a diverse population of students. In addition, Scott loved being manager of the Wheeler High School girls' varsity basketball team for four years. As part of the team, he provided the girls with ice and water at every home and away game. His participation in this sport not only taught him responsibility but also improved his social skills. Motivating your brother or sister to participate in extracurricular activities is a great way to get them involved in the community.

Private schools are also really cool for kids with special needs because they have fewer students and allow our brothers and sisters to get more attention from their teachers and with fewer distractions in the classroom. It is more important to keep in mind that there are many educational options to explore for our siblings with special needs.

Does Scott have a girlfriend? Will he ever get married?

Scott likes girls just as much as any other guy; however, his relationships with girls have not been very serious. I am not sure if Scott will ever get married. I guess marriage could be a possibility if he found the right girl.

What kind of support is Scott going to need as he gets older?

Scott will definitely need more support from his family and friends than most people. For example, Scott will never be able to balance a checkbook by himself or handle emergency situations. He will need someone to assist him to live independently. Additionally, he will always need help making plans to go out with his friends; otherwise, he would stay home all day long,

My oldest brother, Jared, and I have discussed the additional attention Scott will need. In the past, our parents have watched over Scott to make sure he was always happy and comfortable. However, as we get older, Scott's well-being will become more our responsibility. Fortunately, Jared and I plan to settle near Scott and remain an active part of his life.

Family support is essential for our extra special siblings; it's important that they know we will always be there for them. Although this appears to be an extra responsibility, our brothers and sisters are certainly worth it.

Does Scott know he has fragile X?

The answer is yes, and he is proud of it. I credit much of Scott's high self-esteem to my parents. My parents are the strong roots of the family tree from which three awesome kids have sprung. My parents have always been supportive, loving, and available for all three of us.

Scott knows he has fragile X syndrome. My parents told Scott about his disorder in such a way that he feels that he is the luckiest, most special boy alive. Scott probably does not know what fragile X is scientifically, but he does know he has it and he is happy in that knowledge.

There is one story my family will treasure forever. Several years ago, we were in the car, and Jared was asking my parents about fragile X. He had just learned that fragile X is a genetic disorder, carried in the genes. Curious to know if Scott had picked up on this concept, Jared asked, "Scott, what's in your genes?" Scott looked down, thought for a moment, and then proudly responded, "Underwear!" These innocent, adorable responses make Scott so special.

Later, I was curious as to what Scott knew about fragile X. I asked, "Scott, what makes you so special?" As expected, he responded with, "Fragile X." Then I asked, "But what if I want to be special, too?" He looked at me with a smile and responded, "Go see Dr. Stephanie. She has fragile X, and if you ask her nicely, she'll give you some." That was the best answer I could have received. It showed that Scott was willing to share the most special part of himself with me—his fragile X.

Dr. Stephanie Sherman is a good friend and a well-known genetic researcher specializing in fragile X syndrome at Emory University School of Medicine. She has worked closely with our family and has helped us learn about fragile X through her research. Obviously, Scott is pretty fond of Stephanie and knows she "has" fragile X—perhaps even enough to share. I told Scott that his was a great idea!

Do you ever think Scott gets more attention because he is special?

There are times when Scott gets more attention than I do, but that is because he requires it. There are also times when I need more attention from my parents, and I get it. Being anyone's sibling—and especially of someone with special needs—teaches us about patience and sharing. These qualities help keep families together and are useful for everyday encounters in life.

Instead of getting frustrated when your parents give extra attention to your brother or sister, try to be patient and know that there are also times when you will need extra attention. Also, ask your parents if they ever need your help. I am sure they would appreciate the offer. Try to be the best sibling you can be.

Do you ever wonder what Scott would be like if he did not have fragile X?

Yes, I have often wondered what he would look like, how he would act, or what he would be interested in. I have also wondered what my life would be like if I did not have my eXtra-special brother. Would I have such a great passion for people who are mentally challenged or be as understanding of them as I am today?

When I was younger, I thought it was bad for me to think these thoughts. However, as I have gotten older, I have realized it is only natural to be curious about such things. Although these thoughts still wander through my head, I have a constant love for Scott no matter how he looks or acts. Scott is my older brother—whether or not he has fragile X.

Do you ever wish Scott did not have fragile X?

When I was younger, I wished Scott were different more than I do today. Sometimes I became angry or frustrated with Scott simply because I did not understand him or know how to deal with him. I wanted Scott to be just like my oldest brother, Jared. I thought it would be the coolest thing to have two "real" older brothers. I knew Scott was different and I got along with him great, but it wasn't until recently that I opened my eyes to see how much Scott means to me and how much he has taught me. The fact that I have a higher IQ than Scott doesn't mean he can't teach me a thing or two about life.

Writing this book and trying to find the words to help others has allowed me to see the powerful effect Scott has had on my life— an effect that I previously ignored. I hope to help you see the many positive ways your sibling has influenced your life, too.

Try to clear your mind of the embarrassing moments and frustrating times you've experienced with your sibling and focus instead on how much your brother or sister has taught you. I'm sure you'll find more lessons than you realized. For example, I'll bet you are more tolerant of differences than most other kids your age. In addition, you are probably more willing to talk with different types of people regardless of their physical appearance, ability to talk, or even their odd behaviors. Also, you are most likely more capable of managing difficult situations, learning from them, and moving on.

Learning how to live with someone with special needs teaches us beautiful lessons. Be proud of lessons you have learned.

Did You Know...?

An Expert Answers Your Technical Fragile X Questions

What is fragile X syndrome?

This is a genetic condition that leads to a wide range of mental impairment from mild learning disabilities to severe mental retardation. The syndrome is caused by a change in the instructions of a gene called FMR1, which is located on the X chromosome. The location of the gene and its unique effect on the chromosome led to the naming of the syndrome—fragile X.

What is a genetic disorder?

A genetic disorder is caused by change—also known as a mutation—in a human gene. A gene is the basic unit of heredity and is passed from parent to child. A mutation in a gene causes that gene to function abnormally. The most common mutation that leads to fragile X syndrome causes the gene to be shut off and therefore to not make any of the protein called FMRP, which is involved in brain function.

What are other genetic disorders?

Other examples of genetic disorders that come about because of a mutation in a single gene are cystic fibrosis, sickle cell anemia, Tay Sachs disease, and hemophilia. Genes also play a role in many common conditions—such as heart disease and cancer—but are usually not the sole cause of these conditions. Everyone has about five to ten mutations among the thousands of genes they carry. Sometimes they cause problems, or sometimes they are masked by the presence of other genes.

What is a mental impairment?

Mental impairment is a term used to express some discrepancy from the accepted norm regarding a person's mental capacity. This can be caused by many different factors, both genetic and environmental. Depending on the cause, it can "look" very different. Individuals with fragile X syndrome are usually developmentally delayed, which means they don't meet developmental milestones—such as sitting up, walking, or talking—at the same age as other children. They have problems with learning (arithmetic is very hard for them), with motor skills, and with specific types of memory skills. Mental impairment due to other causes may have a very different profile because different parts of the brain may be affected.

How common is fragile X syndrome?

Because the FMR1 gene is located on the X chromosome, boys are more severely affected than girls. People are born with a set of two chromosomes: boys have one X chromosome and one Y chromosome (XY) whereas girls have two X chromosomes (XX). That means that boys have only one copy of the FMR1 gene (because they only have one X chromosome), and girls have two copies (because they have two X chromosomes). If there is a mutation in one gene, it causes the syndrome in boys. In girls, however, the FMR1 gene without the mutation will sometimes mask the effect of the mutation in the other gene. This happens about 70% of the time—that is, only about 30% of girls who carry the mutation in the FMR1 gene have significant symptoms of fragile X syndrome. Fragile X syndrome occurs once in about 4,000 boys and once in about 8,000 girls.

What is a carrier?

A *carrier* is a person who "carries" the mutation that can possibly result in his or her future generations having a child with fragile X syndrome. Carriers do not exhibit any signs of the syndrome.

What is premutation?

It's complicated but important. The mutation leading to fragile X syndrome is unique because it has a feature that many mutations do not: It has an early form that progressively leads to the final mutation that causes fragile X syndrome. The early form does not specifically *cause* fragile X syndrome, but when passed from parent to child, it can change to the final form of the mutation. That early form is called the *premutation*. About 1 in 300 girls and 1 in 1,000 boys carry the premutation form. Those who carry the fragile X mutation in the early or final form have a chance of having a son or daughter with fragile X syndrome. That is, they are "carriers" of fragile X syndrome (see the previous question).

What are the statistics about siblings?

A brother or sister of an individual with fragile X syndrome may or may not carry the premutation (early form) or final form of the mutation that causes fragile X. The sibling's chance of being a carrier of any form of the mutation is 50%. That is, their mother has two X chromosomes, one with the mutation and one without. Every time that mother has a child, there is a 50% chance of passing the one with the mutation and a 50% chance of passing the one without the mutation. It doesn't matter how often the mother has already passed on the mutation causing fragile X—it's still a "flip of the coin" for each one of her children. If the mother does pass on the mutation for fragile X syndrome (again, a 50% chance), it may or may not progress to the final form. So a sibling of an individual with fragile X may not carry the mutation (50% of the time) *or* may carry the premutation or the final form (50% of the time). Every brother and sister will be different no matter what!

What is the life expectancy for people who have fragile X syndrome?

Fragile X syndrome leads to mental impairment but is not associated with any significant medical problems. Therefore, individuals with the fragile X gene lead long and healthy lives, similar to others without the syndrome.

Is there a cure for fragile X syndrome?

No, there is no cure—*yet*. However, ongoing research is attempting to achieve an understanding of the normal functions of the FMR1 gene—exactly what it does, when it needs to be active and in what cells, how it interacts with other proteins, and so on. Once we answer these questions thoroughly, we hope to also understand more about what happens when FMR1 is *not* present (which is the situation with those who have fragile X syndrome). This knowledge will help determine possible treatment points for the specific problems associated with fragile X syndrome and possibly determine if a cure can be developed.

Can you "catch" fragile X syndrome?

No, you can't. The mutation is inherited by the child of the carrier. However, it can be passed unnoticed through many generations in its early form that does not lead to any symptoms associated with fragile X syndrome; these carriers would have no reason to suspect that they carry the mutation.

What about other special needs?

"Special needs" is a catch-all phrase that describes a wide variety of disorders. These may be caused by one gene or many genes, by environmental factors, or by a combination of many factors. About 5% of the population falls into this category, but this percentage can be larger or smaller depending on the current definition of "special needs." Sometimes a "special needs" disorder is inherited, but more often it is not.

Resources

Sources For More Information About Fragile X Syndrome

FRAXA Research Foundation
45 Pleasant Street
Newburyport, MA 01950
Phone: 978-462-1866
Fax: 978-463-9985
Email: info@fraxa.org
http://www.fraxa.org

National Fragile X Foundation
P.O. Box 190488
San Francisco, CA 94119
Phone: 800-688-8765
Fax: 925-938-9315
Email: NATLFX@FragileX.org
http://www.fragilex.org

Fragile X Association of Georgia
Emory University School of Medicine
Department of Human Genetics
615 Michael Street, Suite 301
Atlanta, GA 30322
Phone: 404-727-9393
Fax: 404-727-3949
Email: fragilex@esal.org

Organizations That Work With Children With Special Needs

American Association for People with Disabilities
258 Main St. Suite 203
Milford, MA 01757
Phone: 508-634-3200 (V/TTY) or 866-241-3200
http://www.aapd.com

The Arc of the United States
1010 Wayne Avenue, Suite 650
Silver Spring, MD 20910
Phone: 301-565-3842
Fax: 301-565-3843
http://www.thearc.org/

Asperger Syndrome Information and Support
http://www.udel.edu/bkirby/asperger/

Autism Society of America
7910 Woodmont Avenue, Suite 300
Bethesda, MD 20814-3067
Phone: 301-657-0881 or 1-800-328-8476
Fax: 301-657-0869
Email: info@autism-society.org
http://www.autism-society.org

C.H.A.D.D.
(Children and Adults with Attention Deficit
    Disorder)
8181 Professional Place, Suite 201
Landover, MD 20785
Phone: 800-233-4050 or 310-306-7070
Fax: 301-306-7090
Email: national@chadd.com
http://www.chadd.org

Cornelia de Lange Syndrome Foundation
http://www.cdlsusa.org/

Council for the Exceptional Children (CEC)
1920 Association Drive
Reston, VA 20191
Phone: 800-232-7733 or 703-620-3660
http://www.cec.sped.org

Family Village
Waisman Center
1500 Highland Avenue
Madison, WI 53705
Phone: 608-263-5776
Email: familyvillage@waisman.wisc.edu
http://www.familyvillage.wisc.edu

International Rett Syndrome Association
http://www.rettsyndrome.org/

National Down Syndrome Congress
1370 Center Drive, Suite 102
Atlanta, GA 30338
Phone: 800-232-6372 or 770-604-9500
E-Mail: info@ndsccenter.org
http://www.ndsccenter.org

National Down Syndrome Society
666 Broadway
New York, NY 10012
Phone: 800-221-4602 or 212-460-9330
http://www.ndss.org

National Information Center for Children
    and Youth
P.O. Box 1492
Washington, D.C. 20013
Phone: 800-695-0285 (V/TTY)
Fax: 202-884-8441
Email: nichcy@aed.org
http://www.nichcy.org

National Parent to Parent Support and
    Information System
Internet Special Education Resources
P.O. Box 907
Blue Ridge, GA 30513
Phone: 800-651-1151 (Parents) or
    706-632-8832
Fax: 706-632-8830
Email: Judd103w@wonder.em.cdc.gov
http://www.iser.com/NPPSIS-GA.html

Prader-Willi Syndrome
5700 Midnight Pass Rd.
Sarasota, FL 34242
Phone: 800-926-4797
Fax: 941-312-0142
Email: www.pwsausa.org
http://www.pwsausa.org/index.html

Presidents Committee on Mental Retardation
370 L'Enfant Promenade, SW, Suite 701
Washington, D.C. 20447
Phone: 202-619-0634
Fax: 202-2-5-9519
Email: pcmr@acf.hhs.gov
http://www.acf.dhhs.gov/programs/pcmr

Special Olympics
1325 G Street, NW Suite 500
Washington, D.C. 20005
Phone: 202-628-3630
Fax: 202-824-0200
Email: info@specialolympics.com
http://www.specialolympics.org/

Tourette Syndrome Association
Phone: 718-224-2999
http://www.tsa-usa.org/

Turner's Syndrome Society
http://www.turner-syndrome-us.org/

United Cerebral Palsy
Phone: 1-800-872-5827
Email: national@ucp.org
http://www.ucpa.org/

U.S. Department of Health and Human Services
HHH 300-F, 370 L'Enfant Promenade
Washington, D.C. 20447
Phone: 202-690-6590

Williams Syndrome Association
P.O. Box 297
Clawson, MI 48017-0297
Phone: 800-806-1871
Fax: 248-541-3631
Email: info@williams-syndrome.org
http://www.williams-syndrome.org/

Williams Syndrome Foundation
University of California
Irvine, GA 92679
Phone: 949-824-7259
Email: hlenhoff@uci.edu
http://www.williamssyndrome.org/

Sibling Support Web Sites For Families With Special Needs

Kid Info
http://www.kidinfo.com/

Georgia Deaf-Blind Project Sibling Page
http://education.gsu.edu/georgiadeafblindproj/SIB%20WEB%20PAGE.htm

Sibling Support Project
http://www.thearc.org/siblingsupport/

Special Child
http://www.specialchild.com/

Special Families Resource Center
http://www.specialfamilies.com/special_siblings.htm

Supporting Transition Age Youth with Disabilities
http://www.transitionlink.com

Magazines Of Interest

Exceptional Parent Magazine
http://eparent.com

Parent Magazine
http://parents.com

Photo Gallery

On the following pages are pictures of Scott with his family and friends. These photos capture many of the fun activities and important people in his life. They also show the happiness he brings to others each day.

We hope these pictures will trigger the wonderful memories you have shared with your sibling, too. Remember, the time you spend with family and friends is priceless.

The grown-up Heyman family sitting on the deck. Clockwise from top: Jared, Carly (me), Gail (Mom), Lady, Scott, and Lyons (Dad).

Scott—who could resist such an adorable grin?

Stephanie, our talented illustrator, with Scott at the prom.

Celebrating Scott's accomplishments.

Scott loves bowling—check out that great form!

From left: Scott, Mom, and Jared. I am standing in front with Dominique on my shoulder.

Scott and his friend, Russell, hanging out at a high school basketball game.

Paul, Russell, and Scott, best friends since elementary school.

Paul and Scott, pumped up after attending their favorite wrestling event!

Scott and yours truly enjoying the great outdoors.

Aunt Janet and Mom sending their three eXtra special boys—
Scott, Alan, and Todd—to summer camp.

Three eXtra-special cousins: Scott, Todd, and Alan.

Three eXtra-special cousins, all grown up and still buddies…!

"Hold on, Dad—I'm on the phone!"

Coach Harry gives Scott a thumbs up.   My gold medalist brother!

Our eXtraordinary first cousins at Hilton Head on our annual Thanksgiving family vacation.

Here we are again. Scott is standing on the left; I am sitting on the left.

The "Scott squat" is a perfect position for playing catcher!

Scott, feeling cool, driving the boat.

Scott having a blast paddling on the river.

Baby Scott and Trey—what a pair!

Scott and me, making a face—on a pumpkin!

Our eXceptional eXtended family—together forever.

Ecstatic Scott hugs Dad after returning from
Camp Barney.

Every member of the family has a close relationship with Scott. LEFT: Jared
with his little brother. RIGHT: Mom reads Scott a story book.

Keeping cool isn't always easy in Georgia, even for three very
cool cousins!

Everyone gets silly at times—so here we are, enjoying the moment.

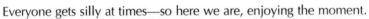

Me and my eXcellent brother.

The Wheeler High School varsity girls' basketball team. Scott, a loyal team manager for four years, is stretching out in the right side of the picture.

I love my brother!

Stephanie and Scott.

Fabulous Favorites

This page will help you and your sibling discover more about each other.
First, fill in your favorites, and then compare them to your sibling's answers.
Or, if you feel up to the challenge, try to fill in each other's responses!

Nickname: _____

Color: _____

Food: _____

Sport: _____

Movie: _____

Song: _____

Pet: _____

Friend: _____

Place: _____

Book: _____

Quote: _____

Fabulous Favorites

This page will help you and your sibling discover more about each other.
First, fill in your favorites, and then compare them to your sibling's answers.
Or, if you feel up to the challenge, try to fill in each other's responses!

Nickname: _____

Color: _____

Food: _____

Sport: _____

Movie: _____

Song: _____

Pet: _____

Friend: _____

Place: _____

Book: _____

Quote: _____

Silly Sibling Stories

I have shared with you many of my silly "Scott stories"—now it's your turn to write down your own silly sibling stories. Use the space below to record the fun experiences you have shared with your sibling!

_____

_____

_____

_____

_____

_____

_____

_____

_____

_____

_____

Silly Sibling Stories

I have shared with you many of my silly "Scott stories"—now it's your turn to write down your own silly sibling stories. Use the space below to record the fun experiences you have shared with your sibling!

Awesome Activities

On this page, write down the awesome activities you enjoy doing with your sibling. Spending time with your family is one of life's greatest pleasures, so take a moment to remember the good times!

_____

_____

_____

_____

_____

_____

_____

_____

_____

_____

Awesome Activities

On this page, write down the awesome activities you enjoy doing with your sibling. Spending time with your family is one of life's greatest pleasures, so take a moment to remember the good times!

Sibling Success

There are hundreds of times when our siblings impress us. On this page, write down the sibling success moments you never want to forget!

_____

_____

_____

_____

_____

_____

_____

_____

_____

_____

Sibling Success

There are hundreds of times when our siblings impress us. On this page, write down the sibling success moments you never want to forget!

Happy Hands

Whose hand is bigger? On these pages, trace each other's hands and compare them. Then sign your name and age so you can remember this time forever. (If your hand is too big for this page, you can use a piece of regular paper.)

Happy Hands

Whose hand is bigger? On these pages, trace each other's hands and compare
them. Then sign your name and age so you can remember this time forever. (If
your hand is too big for this page, you can use a piece of regular paper.)

Picture Perfect

Pictures are perfect for capturing some of the many happy times you share with your sibling. Paste some of your favorite sibling photos here to remind each other of your special bond. Then write your own captions!

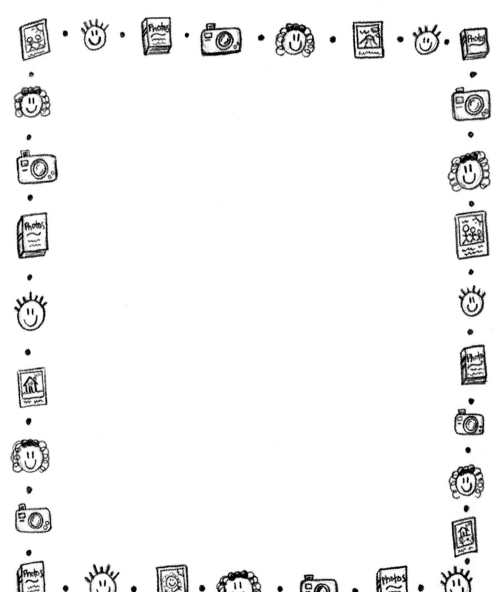

Picture Perfect

Pictures are perfect for capturing some of the many happy times you share with your sibling. Paste some of your favorite sibling photos here to remind each other of your special bond. Then write your own captions!

Picture Perfect

Pictures are perfect for capturing some of the many happy times you share with your sibling. Paste some of your favorite sibling photos here to remind each other of your special bond. Then write your own captions!

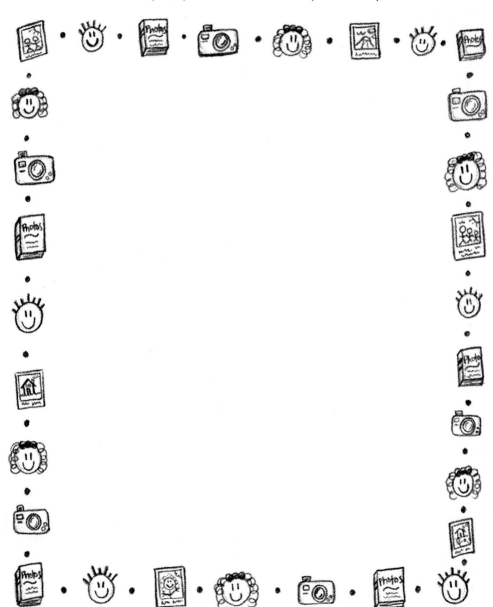

Picture Perfect

Pictures are perfect for capturing some of the many happy times you share with your sibling. Paste some of your favorite sibling photos here to remind each other of your special bond. Then write your own captions!

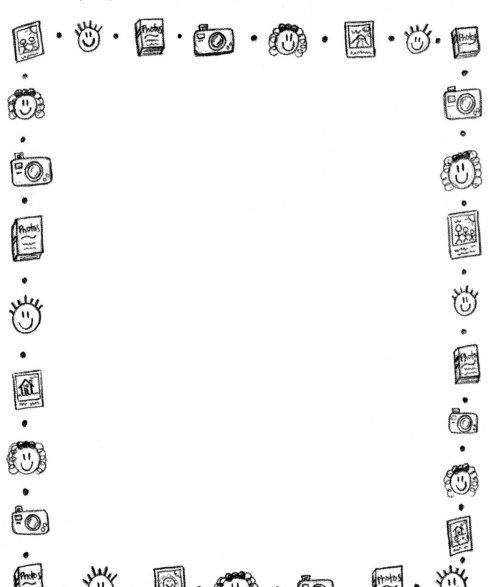

Printed in the United States
880600005B